LONDON UNDERGROUND 1967–99

JOHN GLOVER

AMBERLEY

Front, top: Wembley Park station has six platforms, two of which are for the Jubilee line. A southbound train of 1995 stock from Stanmore is arriving. The overbridges in the background may seem to be surprisingly high, but they do have to offer sufficient clearances for subsurface stock, as well as the Tube stock seen here; *bottom*: With negligible exceptions, the D stock kept this one livery for the whole of their time on London Underground. Other subsequent owners had different ideas. Here, an eastbound train bound for Upminster arrives at Becontree. This is a four-tracked length of railway, with two for National Rail and London Underground respectively.

Back: On 28 December 1996, a train of A stock, still in unpainted aluminium finish, is seen at Dollis Hill on a southbound working to Aldgate. Metropolitan services run non-stop from Wembley Park to Finchley Road over the 7.24 km in 7 minutes; this compares with the 12.5 minutes (or thereabouts) taken by today's Jubilee-line services, with five intermediate stops.

First published 2024

Amberley Publishing
The Hill, Stroud
Gloucestershire, GL5 4EP

www.amberley-books.com

Copyright © John Glover, 2024

The right of John Glover to be identified as the Author of this work has been asserted in accordance with the Copyrights, Designs and Patents Act 1988.

ISBN 978 1 3981 1200 1 (print)
ISBN 978 1 3981 1201 8 (ebook)

British Library Cataloguing in Publication Data. A catalogue record for this book is available from the British Library.

Origination by Amberley Publishing. Printed in the UK.

Introduction

This book covers the period from the construction of the Victoria line in 1967 to the completion of the Jubilee line in 1999. By a very small margin, this latter enabled the then prime minister, Tony Blair, and others to travel on it from Westminster to Stratford for the millennial celebrations.

The post-war years had been a disappointment for London Underground and its customers. Although the Central line extension to West Ruislip was completed in 1948 and those to Epping and Hainault in 1949, that was about it. The Northern line's proposed extension beyond Edgware to Bushey Heath, plus the awaited extension from Mill Hill East, and the acquisition of the Alexandra Palace branch from British Railways never proceeded beyond where they had reached in 1941. All were abandoned in the early 1950s. Great plans for new lines remained ignored by government, though the Metropolitan electrification to Amersham, Chesham and Watford, and its general modernisation, did go ahead eventually. These were completed in 1962.

Rolling stock replacement didn't proceed much better. Further R stock cars were built for the District, and the Metropolitan got its electric A stock for their longer-distance services. A few more cars of 1938 stock were built (classed as 1949 stock), while the Piccadilly received its much needed 1959 stock of seven-car trains. The Central got its very similar 1962 stock, but of eight cars.

The general lack of progress was enlivened only by the electrification of the Central line's remote Epping–Ongar branch in 1957 (as nobody could think of anything better to do with it) and the rebuilding of Notting Hill Gate as a combined station for the Central and District/Circle lines in 1959. The same year also saw the closure of the District's short and self-contained Acton Town to South Acton branch. There was also the opening of a re-sited Tower Hill station on the District and Circle lines in 1967.

Technical developments saw the installation of programme machines for junction setting at Kennington in 1958, while automatic ticket barriers were installed at Stamford Brook in 1964. This was the same year in which trials of automatic train operation (ATO) on the Woodford–Hainault section of the Central line began.

This last was a necessary component of the substantially automated Victoria line, Walthamstow Central to (eventually) Brixton, for which the Macmillan government gave approval in 1962. This entirely new line was aimed at relieving the most congested parts of the Underground in central London, which had remained virtually unchanged since it was built in the years leading up to the First World War. It would also help the government by reducing unemployment.

The illustrations in this volume show views of the Underground as it appeared from 1967 until the end of the twentieth century.

In the post-war years, passengers had not flocked to the Underground. Using the measure of passenger km per year in millions (the multiple of the number of passenger journeys and the average distance travelled), the first post-nationalisation year of 1948 saw 6.2 million passenger km. But this number slowly dwindled, to the extent that by 1978 this was down to 4.5 million.

A decade later, in 1988, passenger numbers were back to 6.3 million and growth continued, reaching 8.5 million passenger km by 2008/09. A prolonged rise in volumes saw 12.1 million passenger km in 2018/19. This was followed by an unprecedented loss of passengers in 2020/21, and subsequently, due to the Covid-19 pandemic. There are now encouraging signs, but how matters might develop in the long-term future remains an open question.

* * * * *

This book is divided into sections, starting with line-by-line pictures of the Metropolitan, Widened Lines, Hammersmith & City and Circle, District and East London lines. These are followed by the tube lines, in alphabetical order.

It continues with pictures of the engineering fleets, some museum items and vehicles on preserved railways, finishing with the Isle of Wight and its now long-standing connections with London Transport railways.

All photographs are by the author. Those within depots or similar were either taken on public open days, or on professional visits accompanied by London Underground staff.

John Glover, February 2024

Metropolitan Railway

This is the final version of the Metropolitan Railway coat of arms as used up to the time of the company's demise in 1933. It was displayed on rolling stock and elsewhere, and featured the shields of the City of London, the now defunct County of Middlesex, Buckinghamshire and Hertfordshire, through all of which the Metropolitan passed. The fist emitting sparks is understood to signify electrification.

The Moorgate/Barbican area needed total reconstruction in the post-war era. This included straightening the 500 metres of railway between those stations, crucial for the Barbican development. This view shows Moorgate station in 1967. It was yet to be built over and shows an A stock train to Uxbridge and a Class 31 locomotive on a Great Northern Widened Lines service.

An A stock train in corporate livery arrives at Farringdon with a westbound Metropolitan train to Uxbridge. This is a large station with an impressive overall roof. Out of view to the right are the tracks of the Widened Lines, which were built for the benefit of trains from other companies, while keeping the Metropolitan tracks clear for their intended users. It is 22 March 1998.

This April 1998 view shows a Metropolitan main-line service with an A stock train arriving at Farringdon, bound for Aldgate. The pedestrian bridge is that linking the four platforms, thus avoiding the need for interchange passengers to use the only other bridge which would take them close to the station's entry and exit routes.

This is Baker Street station looking towards Finchley Road, with the platforms for main-line Metropolitan trains. A stock trains in their original unpainted aluminium livery are shown. Platform 1 (far left) is a terminal platform; the arriving terminating train is routed into Platform 2. This is used also for trains originating from Aldgate and continuing to suburban destinations.

On the eastern side of Baker Street main-line platforms in this March 1998 view is the 1913 signal box. This housed a power frame together with AC track circuiting and electric signalling. It used Westinghouse Brake & Saxby signal equipment and their point machines to control the line northwards from Baker Street City Junction towards Harrow.

These Metropolitan platforms at Baker Street have some sections in the open air. This view of March 1998 shows an A stock train departing from Platform 2 and another in Platform 3 about to leave for Aldgate. Corporate livery does help to brighten up what would otherwise be rather dismal surroundings.

May 1988 sees an unpainted A stock train bound for Watford on the approaches to Willesden Green station in May 1988. The overbridges in the background seem to have avoided having their right-hand span painted. Perhaps this was an economically minded British Rail responsibility, whereas the others were that of London Transport?

The Metropolitan opened Neasden station as Kingsbury & Neasden on 2 April 1880, renaming it Neasden & Kingsbury on 1 January 1910. It became plain Neasden on 1 January 1932, with the Kingsbury name transferred to the first station north of Wembley Park on the new Stanmore branch. This opened on 10 December 1932. Bakerloo services used Neasden's centre platforms from 20 November 1939, becoming the Jubilee from 1 May 1979. This is a March 1998 view, looking towards Baker Street.

An A stock train from the Harrow-on-the-Hill direction is bound for Uxbridge in March 1998 and is seen at Rayners Lane Junction where the Piccadilly line joins the Metropolitan. The two lines proceed together over 8.7 km of double track to the terminus, serving a total of seven stations on the way.

Rayners Lane station building is seen from the platforms, looking towards the junction where Metropolitan trains take the left-hand route, and the Piccadilly the right. The station was rebuilt following the general style of Sudbury Town, but a few years later, in 1938. An A stock train for Aldgate stands in the eastbound platform.

This is the interior of an A stock car, showing how three-plus-two seating was arranged each side of an off-centre gangway. This was helped by the vehicle width being a generous 9 feet 8 inches (2,946 mm), which allowed the seating to be rather more comfortable than might otherwise have been the case. Note the provision of luggage racks, a rare facility on the Underground.

An A stock train for Uxbridge passes the by now non-operational signal box as it approaches Ruislip station in February 1997. Rather than being demolished, alternative uses for such buildings, and there are several throughout the Underground, are often found should they become redundant. Waste not, want not.

The construction of the M40 motorway required access roads, which at the southern end was to be routed from the A40, then below the Metropolitan's line and station at Hillingdon. The station itself was moved about a train's length further west, and this view shows the rebuilt platforms in February 1997 with a train in the distance. This work included the provision of a much-enlarged car park.

On the main line, North Harrow is the first of three stations to have platforms on the local lines only. It was opened in 1915. The facilities might be described as basic, but there are plenty of seats. There is a sad shortage of passengers on the southbound platform, seen here. An A stock train is approaching on 11 April 1998.

Beyond Watford South Junction, the branch to Watford (Met) leaves the main line. East of Croxley, this is the railway bridge with an A stock train crossing the Grand Union Canal. This view of March 1998 looks south along the canal towards Rickmansworth. Proposals to close the last section of this branch and re-route it to Watford Junction now seem unlikely to happen.

A Chiltern Railways service on the Down line (or should it be called the northbound?) approaches Chalfont & Latimer on 31 April 1998. All services for Great Missenden, Wendover, Stoke Mandeville and Aylesbury have been provided by British Railways, or their successors Chiltern Railways, since September 1961. Aylesbury itself can also be reached by Chiltern via Princes Risborough.

Chalfont & Latimer station building on the Up side of the main line and as seen on 13 April 1998 is a somewhat forbidding affair, but it fulfils its purpose adequately. Rather unusually, the only pedestrian link between the two platforms, which are both directly accessible from a road, is by subway.

A southbound A stock train to Aldgate is arriving at Chalfont & Latimer on 13 April 1998. On the right is a four-car unit which will form the branch service. That is no longer possible, as all trains are now formed of S8 stock. It was here in 2020 that a head-on collision nearly took place with a southbound Chiltern train that did not comply with the signals. It traversed the crossover and stopped 23 metres short of a Metropolitan train to Chesham, waiting to depart.

Chesham is at the end of the single-track branch of 3 miles 74 chains (6.35 km) from Chalfont & Latimer; it was reached by the Metropolitan Railway on 8 July 1889. The four-car shuttle of A stock is arriving on 13 April 1998. On electrification in 1961 a new bay platform was provided, but all trackwork apart than that serving the single passenger platform has now been removed.

Metropolitan services continued to Aylesbury until completion of the much-delayed electrification to Amersham. Since then, services beyond have been the sole responsibility of British Railways and their successors. Here a less than pristine Network SouthEast diesel unit No. 165.023 forms an Up service to London Marylebone as it arrives at Great Missenden on 11 April 1998.

The Metropolitan Railway continued to the rural outpost of Verney Junction, 50.5 miles from Baker Street, where it met the one-time Oxford to Cambridge line of British Railways. The Metropolitan became part of London Transport in 1933 and this appendage was closed, without delay, in 1936. Built as a double-track railway, this is a 1994 view along a former cutting.

Widened Lines, Hammersmith & City, Circle

The Widened Lines consisted of a double-track line from King's Cross St Pancras to Moorgate, first on the north, then on the south side, of the Metropolitan tracks. Here dual voltage unit No. 319.425 is seen at Moorgate, with a Midland service to Luton. The open space above the tracks was retained to allow diesel exhaust fumes to escape.

This is Barbican and the two tracks to the right are those of the Widened Lines. This is a Midland service from Moorgate to Luton with No. 317.302 leading. Platform width at the ends was very restricted, a real problem when eight-car trains were introduced. The section east of Farringdon is currently disused, following the introduction of cross-London Thameslink services via Blackfriars.

This C stock train is at Barbican on an inner-rail Circle line working in March 1998. It is bedecked with Yellow Pages advertising. Such overall advertising on Underground trains was only used in a few instances and is no longer being applied. It did not seem to meet with much enthusiasm by the public and Yellow Pages no longer exists anyway.

Rounding the curve into Farringdon station from the east is a C stock train in corporate livery bound for Hammersmith via Shepherd's Bush. Curvature on urban lines such as this can often be very tight indeed, with consequential results in terms of wheel flange wear, perhaps with accompanying noise and speed restrictions. The Widened Lines can be seen to the right in this picture of March 1998.

There is little mistaking the twenty-five stations of the Metropolitan Railway which were designed by the company's architect, Charles Walter Clark. This is a street view of Farringdon, showing its reconstruction dating from 1922. Other notable examples, all listed, are Great Portland Street (1912), Baker Street (1911–13), Paddington (1915), Willesden Green (1925), Croxley (1925) and Watford (1925).

Farringdon station platforms are all curved, which itself can be a problem since it results in greater stepping distances when joining or alighting from trains. A westbound Circle line train consisting of refurbished C stock is arriving in June 2000. Being intended primarily for short-distance urban use, these trains had four pairs of double doors per vehicle side to reduce station stop times. It also reduced seating capacity.

Looking south from Bayswater station platforms, the waiting passenger gets a good view of the retaining walls. These are used on the subsurface lines to keep the operational railway secure. Mechanical construction methods then were still much in their infancy. The approaching C stock train is a District service from Wimbledon to Edgware Road. It is 28 April 1997.

At High Street Kensington, although the station is below ground level, it is largely in open air. A C stock Circle line train on the Inner Rail is arriving in June 1990. These were ordered from Metro-Cammell in two batches of 212 vehicles (the C69 stock) and a further sixty-seven cars (the C77 stock). Their service life extended from 1970 to 2014, when they were replaced by S7 stock.

Going west from Edgware Road is the route of the Hammersmith & City. A train of that line is seen in Paddington Platform 15, with a Class 122 unit of Network SouthEast in the adjoining Platform 14. It is August 1990. This was not always a happy inter-operator arrangement. Physically, the tracks of each are now completely separate and there are no conflicting junctions.

Westbourne Park was once used as a 'transfer station' for passengers moving to or from what is now the Hammersmith & City line. The British Railways part closed on 16 March 1992. Here, in August 1989, an eastbound C stock train is about to use the dive under to gain the north side of the Great Western tracks and the Underground stations at Royal Oak and Paddington.

This is a May 1995 view of Hammersmith Depot with its eleven roads. On the right is the road with the carriage washer. All the trains are C stock, which provided all services on the Hammersmith & City, the Circle line and for Edgware Road–Wimbledon trains (part of the District). The last C stock train ran in passenger service in June 2014.

It was perhaps unfortunate that the Hammersmith terminus of the H&C was built where it was, with two busy roads to be crossed by pedestrians, before reaching what became the site of the District & Piccadilly station, but so be it. To judge by the length of the station frontage, one might expect to find more than three tracks and their associated platforms inside. The date is 23 May 1995.

District Line

At the eastern end of the District line is London Underground's push-button-controlled Upminster signal box. It was brought into use on 20 November 1958 and is located at the station platform ends with access direct from a station footbridge. This is where the tracks for the then new stabling and maintenance facility begin.

Arriving at Upminster in June 1979 is a train of R stock, which was operational from 1949 to 1983. It ran on the District line generally, but this excluded the western end of the Circle for clearance and platform length reasons. It formed part of the post-war programme to replace the remaining trains, which had hand-operated sliding doors.

The District line was re-equipped with new D stock between 1979 and 1981, seen here at the same position as on page 23 when entering Upminster station in October 1990. There are three separate railways here. To the north of the three Underground platforms is the Overground line to Romford, and to the south the London, Tilbury & Southend line. All are now electrified.

An eastbound D stock train enters Plaistow, one of the few stations with a reversing facility on the far platform. This enables trains to be turned short of line destination. This of course also requires a crossover to return trains to the westbound direction. The track in the foreground seems to undergo a sharp twist as it passes under the bridge. It is 24 December 1996.

Plaistow station has been served by the District Railway since 2 June 1902. Built originally by the London, Tilbury & Southend company, it latterly had four tracks, each with platforms. Tracks on the south side (right) are now for the exclusive use of National Rail and the platforms are disused. Those on the north are for the District line; the station is operated by London Underground.

Earl's Court Platform 2 sees a C stock train arriving with a train from Wimbledon to Edgware Road. This station retains its magnificent roof, spanning the four tracks and two island platforms. On the right can be seen an R stock train, with its lower body sides curved outwards. This was to discourage those who thought there might be a foothold here, from using it in an attempt to get aboard.

This view of the western end of Earl's Court station from the now demolished Exhibition Centre building sees a westbound D stock train leaving Platform 3. As is so often the case, it emphasises the tight geometry of Underground lines and the impossibility of subsequent sideways expansion, should it be needed for any purpose.

High Street Kensington has two dead-end platform tracks. A D stock train is seen arriving in May 1990. These tracks are used to terminate the Exhibition shuttle service from here to Earl's Court and Kensington Olympia when operative. Alternative rail access to Olympia is now available using London Overground services from Clapham Junction, West Brompton or Willesden Junction.

A Wimbledon-bound D stock train is seen here leaving West Brompton in May 2001. The West London line can just be seen to the right. The two additional platforms here, with access only via the existing Underground station and not directly from the street, were opened on 30 May 1999. The previous main line West Brompton on a nearby site was closed in 1940.

Fulham Broadway station is now entered via a shopping centre, not directly from the street. Much of the previously existing structure has been built over or put to new uses. This 1982 view shows the north end of the station as it was from the footbridge, with a D stock train approaching on a service to Wimbledon.

By the time it reaches Parsons Green station, the railway is elevated above street level, and continues thus to Putney Bridge station and across the River Thames to East Putney. On 28 April 1997 a D stock train is seen arriving with a train to Wimbledon. These were the only examples of sub-surface stock to acquire partial red ends, which certainly made them more visible.

October 1990 sees a C stock train from Edgware Road as it reaches Platform 2 at Wimbledon – its final destination. In doing so, it leaves London Underground property and entered (in those days) that of British Railways. Wimbledon is a station used by Underground services, but not in their ownership. There are, for instance, no roundels anywhere in sight.

Gunnersbury is today a junction for London Overground and District line trains. An eastbound D stock train is leaving. With connections to what was the Southern Railway long since gone, this station once had around five platforms instead of the single island which survives today. The rest was filled with many car parking spaces, which might be useful for those in the large office building in the background.

Turnham Green station has the attribute of platforms on all four lines, assuming that the Piccadilly line trains will be stopping. Selective non-stopping can produce its own difficulties! This station can be popular for interchanging passengers, and a substantial number are about to join this D stock District train arriving on Platform 4 in February 1998. It is bound for Dagenham East.

East London Line

The rolling stock used on the East London line always seemed to be what was left over and not needed (or wanted) anywhere else. It was also limited to four-car train lengths. A mixed bag of subsurface Q rolling stock is seen arriving at Whitechapel low-level Platform 6 with a Shoreditch to New Cross Gate service. The older vehicles have an upper row of windows known as clerestory roofs.

Looking south from the Whitechapel East London line platforms, modernity is not what came to mind. Underground trains first served them from 31 March 1913, although main-line trains had used them from 9 April 1876. A new era opened under London Overground, whose direct operations from here now extend to Highbury & Islington, New Cross, Crystal Palace and Clapham Junction.

The shallow nature of the East London line tunnels is demonstrated here with a southbound train at Shadwell. The bright and cheerful colour scheme latterly applied to the A stock had a very positive effect in situations such as these. Note the disused length of platform; varying platform lengths from station to station provide nothing but operational problems. It is 18 April 1998.

A potential answer to the graffiti problem was to revert to a painted livery, but what should this look like? The East London line was chosen to experiment with some alternatives. Here is an A stock formation. An off-white body with blue doors, including the driver's cab, is coupled with what became the universally applied red ends. It is being shown off at New Cross on 3 May 1990.

The off-white body and blue doors livery (but off-white cab door here), plus red ends, certainly stood out, but it still seemed likely to attract graffiti. The A stock train in this livery, sponsored by the London Docklands Development Corporation, is approaching Canal Junction on 3 May 1990. Livery may be less obvious with an Underground railway, but in reality large chunks of the operation are in the open air.

A high-level vantage point in the Canal Junction area showed off this experimental livery on 27 April 1990. Notably, painting the doors in a contrasting shade makes them much more conspicuous for everybody, and this was quickly seen as a feature to be retained. Perhaps the general effect was a reminder of the British Rail coaching stock livery from 1964.

Another blue and off-white possibility was seen in this train, photographed at Surrey Quays station on 21 April 1990. Passengers on the platforms cannot easily locate the position of the doors, and concentrating the light-coloured panels on the bottom of the car is also the area that is likely to be the quickest to become dirty.

This is all that remained of Shoreditch station, with the former southbound platform (left) still in place but with neither track nor passenger access. An A stock train in what turned out to be close to the final livery, but with a white rather than grey roof, has arrived on 3 May 1990. In its final days, services here were restricted to Monday to Friday peaks and for the nearby Sunday morning market.

Shoreditch station became a single platform on a dead end stretch of track from Whitechapel. It was permanently closed on 9 June 2006. No longer would cash-strapped commuters be seen hurrying up Bishopsgate to the City and their employment; for those coming from the east or south-east this was a (valid) tactic to pay only Zone 2 fares, rather than Zone 1.

This view shows the Great Eastern main line from the end of the Shoreditch platform. Yes, the connection could be (and was) easily made, but to what purpose? Further filling up Liverpool Street main-line platforms was hardly a desirable objective, and it didn't lead anywhere else. Today, the East London line runs via Shoreditch High Street, then linking with the lines which once started from Broad Street, North London line.

Bakerloo Line

Bakerloo line trains have terminated at Harrow & Wealdstone from 4 June 1984, though the two reversing sidings (now only one) were long established. A 1938 stock train will shortly be providing a southbound service. The tracks that continue were for British Rail DC trains to Watford Junction. In the background is the AC wiring for main-line services. It is July 1984.

Stonebridge Park station sees a 1972 Mk II train arriving on the northbound in May 1990. The Bakerloo line depot is adjacent. The platform architecture suggests that the majority of passengers travel towards London – hence the comprehensive canopy for those waiting. Those arriving have lesser facilities, but when they get off their train they go straight home anyway.

North of Willesden Junction station in May 1990, a 1972 Mk II stock train is arriving from Harrow & Wealdstone. This is on the tracks owned by British Railways and shared with their Watford Junction DC service. The tracks to the right link the West Coast main line to the North London line at Kensal Rise.

In May 1990, a 1972 Mk II train arrives at Queen's Park with a train for Elephant & Castle. The Bakerloo uses the two inner platforms: British Rail the two outer. The only route into this platform requires the train to do so via the depot beyond – it is just in picture. This can either be from a depot terminating road or via the connection from the British Rail DC Electric Lines. It is May 1990.

Some Bakerloo line stations display many aspects of their history. This platform level image of Regent's Park shows the Leslie Green tiling and the general approach. Notably, the platform is completely straight, which is always a desirable feature where it can be accommodated. The station was opened on 10 March 1906, but the fluorescent lighting came rather later.

Emergency stairs, as seen here, were provided at Regent's Park for use if required. Lifts were available for passengers, but the reliability of early examples was sometimes a little suspect. It was still too early for the introduction of the escalator. Passenger access and ventilation were two important requirements to be solved, as well as traction for trains, before deep level tube stations could be introduced.

A modest batch of sidings was provided at the Bakerloo's London Road depot, reached using a scissors crossover and then a spur between Waterloo and Lambeth North stations. In this view, two trains of 1938 stock and one of 1959 stock are all that are not being used during the late morning peak. The Bakerloo did not otherwise reach the surface until Queen's Park or Finchley Road.

Central Line

History resulted in the eastern end of the Central line having an unusual layout in which trains from central London to Hainault faced back towards London when they arrived at Woodford. Using otherwise redundant 1960 rolling stock with an additional centre trailer, the branch shuttle on the 6.05-km journey from Hainault stands in Woodford's southbound Platform 2.

Having arrived in Woodford's Platform 2, the shuttle train moved forward to a reversing siding, from which it could be driven directly, when wanted, into Platform 1 for the journey back to Hainault. It is June 1990. The branch was very much a victim of green belt legislation. How many people could have been housed in the vicinity of its stations had matters worked out differently?

The branch was used as a test ground for automatic train operation, and a Victoria line 1967 stock train is seen at Chigwell station on the eastbound Outer Rail. These trains are not normally seen in daylight other than at their Northumberland Park depot. It is not in public service. More recently, branch trains have been provided by extending to Woodford services that would otherwise have terminated at Hainault.

This is one of the three-car 1960 stock trains emerging from the 240-metre Grange Hill Tunnel. It will shortly reach the branch station of that name en route from Woodford to Hainault. It is plain to see that this was constructed for full-sized main-line trains, but even the occasional freights have nowadays been absent for over half a century. It is May 1990.

The Epping–Ongar branch was acquired by London Transport from British Railways, electrified in 1957 and closed in 1994. At its peak, the loop here at North Weald enabled two trains to provide the service. It is seen on 22 July 1977 with a four-car train of 1962 stock to Ongar. The loop line was still in place but disused. That meant a single-track branch shuttle only.

Loughton station is a 1940 rebuild by the London & North Eastern Railway in anticipation of the line's transfer to London Transport's jurisdiction. In reality, this did not happen until 1948, The arched window is made of glass bricks. Inside, there are two island platforms, each with a track on the outer face, and a shared centre track used for train reversals.

Barkingside station, a Great Eastern Railway construction, was opened on 1 May 1903. This is the view from the westbound platform. In classical style, it was huge for a relatively small village community. However, it was also close to the Barnardo's Garden Village, which by 1900 was housing 1,500 girls. Visitors (by train) included royalty.

At Newbury Park there was provision for train reversals in the two centre sidings north of the platform area, seen here in June 1990. After leaving the station, the approaching westbound train of 1962 stock will take the 1940s tunnel under the A12 Eastern Avenue and emerge 5.85 km and three stations later, just short of the former Great Eastern station of Leytonstone.

Newbury Park station was opened on 1 May 1903 by the Great Eastern Railway and substantially rebuilt by the London & North Eastern Railway. It passed to London Transport, who opened it for Underground traffic on 14 December 1947. Notable are the extensive platform canopies, suggesting that substantial passenger growth was expected.

Outside Newbury Park is this Grade II listed bus station. The passenger entrance to the Underground station proper is from the pavement on the far side, and at the far end. It is December 1996. Such a construction may win architectural awards, but from the point of view of those waiting for buses, it is not the place to be on a cold, wet and windy night.

The scale of the bus station building can be more readily appreciated if there is a bus present. Here, a double-deck to Romford station on route 66 is demonstrating just how much clearance the roof provides. Newbury Park is just off the A12 Eastern Avenue, so there is good bus to Underground access, and it takes the buses clear of the main road.

Redbridge station was one of the last Charles Holden creations and opened on 14 December 1947. As the platforms are only slightly below ground level, the station was constructed by using the cut-and-cover method. Between 1942 and 1945 the uncompleted Central line tunnels provided a safe place for around 2,000 people undertaking wartime work.

The Hainault line joins the main line from Epping and Woodford at Leytonstone. The 1962 stock train is coming from the Epping direction. The line from Hainault rises from the tunnel on the right; tracks in the opposite direction can be seen on the left. Leytonstone has an island platform on the westbound side, so that trains from both lines can arrive together.

Bank station on the Central line has tightly curved platforms, which have their own problems in terms of stepping distances. The line's builders kept the tunnels beneath public roads, rather than buildings, to minimise the risk of subsidence claims. On the surface, it can be seen how Poultry and Threadneedle Street relate. A westbound train of 1992 stock is seen here on 18 October 1999.

East Acton station is above ground level, and the eastbound platform has a period waiting room, which can be seen here. The station was opened on 3 August 1920 and was one of the intermediate stations on the Central line extension to Ealing Broadway. A 1992 stock train in the distance is seen approaching on 27 March 1995.

A westbound Central line train of 1962 stock is approaching North Acton station; the bridge in the background carries the North London line. This view of a 1962 stock train shows that it is made up from two four-car units. Each of these was 61.84 metres in length and seated 164 passengers. They continued in service until 11 November 1999.

At North Acton Junction, a 1962 stock train is joining the main part of the Central line from Ealing Broadway; the other branch is from West Ruislip. On the British Rail lines alongside, aggregates empties, perhaps from the Tarmac stone terminal, are heading towards High Wycombe. This route, once part of the former Great Western line to Birmingham, is now severed at the Old Oak Common end.

The Central line station at Greenford has a bay at the London end, from which National Rail services depart. The two sets of tracks are wholly separated. Seen here is a Network SouthEast single unit diesel, No. L122 (55022), performing the service as it was in October 1990. Destinations have varied from London Paddington to Ealing Broadway and (now) West Ealing.

From a similar Greenford viewpoint, a Central line 1962 stock train is arriving with a train from West Ruislip in August 1990. It may be noted that the semaphore signals on the British Rail line to the right appear in both pictures. The bay platform allows doors on both sides of the Ealing Broadway train to be used, but now only if they are released by the train staff.

In July 1985, the original British Railways 'sausage sign' was still in evidence outside West Ruislip station, plus an Underground roundel for the terminus of the Central line. Continuation of the Central line to Denham (in Buckinghamshire rather than Greater London) never took place following green belt planning restrictions.

West Ruislip Central line station has decidedly cramped platform width, when compared with the main-line platforms seen to the right. This picture of 15 March 1997 shows a 1992 stock train, all eight cars of it, being made ready to depart. But this was not intended to be the final terminus. The Underground part of West Ruislip was opened on 21 November 1948.

This diagram of Central line stations served greeted passengers as they descended the stairs to reach West Ruislip platforms in July 1985. It will be noted that reference to Blake Hall, closed 31 October 1981, has been erased, but the rest of the Epping–Ongar line, closed 30 September 1994, is correctly still in situ. A 1962 stock train awaits its passengers.

Central line Driving Motor No. 1631 of 1962 stock finds itself raised for inspection and maintenance work at Ruislip, the line's overhaul depot, on 15 March 1997. A maximum of around seventy-one eight-car trains was required for the Monday to Friday service. End-to-end journey time from West Ruislip to Epping was around 1hr 30 mins, serving a total of thirty-seven stations. Ealing Broadway to Hainault took about 1hr 08 mins, for thirty-one stations.

Ruislip depot hosts Central line trains on a regular basis and 1992 stock with Driving Motor No. 91241 is leading the formation. To the right is a brand-new Jubilee line train of 1996 stock, with Driving Motor No. 96019 leading. It is 15 March 1997. The ability to compare the profiles of two different types of stock in close up happens relatively rarely; the 1992 stock has much straighter sides.

Jubilee Line

The Stanmore station building of 1932 for the Metropolitan was situated on an overbridge. This was designed to allow easy continuation of the line under the A410 to reach wherever any future housing might be developed. A connecting bus, in this case a H12 for South Harrow station, is on offer for any passengers wishing to make use of it. It is April 1998.

At Stanmore on 11 April 1998, a pair of 1996 stock trains stand at the two-platform station of 1932; a third was to be built on the western (left) side in 2011. To the right are stabling sidings. This view shows how limiting two terminal platforms can be; another train approaching has to wait until the train on the left (displaying headlights) has departed and it can be accepted.

The 1983 stock was built for the Jubilee line and a southbound train is seen here arriving at Queensbury on 28 December 1996. These dated from the days when Underground traffic was declining and single-leaf doors were deemed sufficient. But traffic levels recovered and the loading and unloading of passengers was seen as being too slow. The whole of this fleet was withdrawn by 1998.

At Wembley Park, a 1983 stock train arrives from Stanmore in Platform 4 with a southbound service for Charing Cross in June 1988. Further south from here, the Jubilee line trains take the two more central tracks, which are sometimes the only ones with platforms. The Metropolitan line, usually non-stop to Finchley Road, uses the outer two.

A 1983 stock train forms a southbound service as it arrives at Neasden on 28 December 1996. The bridge in the background carries the A406 North Circular Road, while the front of the train shows the effects of graffiti. This was a recurrent problem, solved by quick attention but also by the adoption of the red, white and blue corporate livery throughout the fleet.

The interior of the 1983 stock was similar to many others; this view was taken at Dollis Hill on 28 December 1996. Further use was sought for the stock when withdrawn, but to no avail. The single doors were a major stumbling block; if they were to be converted to a double-door layout, the cost would be such that new trains would be only marginally more expensive.

In the approach to Willesden Green is a 1983 stock train on 4 May 1988. Their six-car length and internal layout enabled the provision of 288 seats or forty-eight per car. This compares with the 234 seats in their 1996 stock replacements, as built, but a seventh car added subsequently brought the 1996 stock seating up to 273.

Having crossed the bridge over the North London line, a 1983 stock train descends towards West Hampstead on 28 December 1996. Between the southbound and northbound lines there is a siding where trains from the south may be terminated. Note that the siding points do not have to be changed for an arriving train, but they do need to be set and locked for departures.

This 1983 stock train eeks out its last days in April 1998, dumped in a siding at Watford (Met), before being removed for scrapping. Heavily vandalised, its positioning in full view of a station platform open to the public was not perhaps the best possible advertisement for the system. One Driving Motor Car has been preserved in the London Transport Museum's depot at Ealing.

The 1938 stock continued to provide passenger services on the Bakerloo line until the 1980s. Here, one such train for Elephant & Castle (but with only Elephant shown on the destination indicator) is arriving on the southbound line at West Hampstead in 1977. Remarkably, the last of these venerable trains was still providing commercial services on the Isle of Wight until 2021.

A train of 1972 Mk II stock calls at West Hampstead with a southbound train to Charing Cross. These thirty-three trains, allocated originally to the Northern line when new in 1974, were transferred to the Bakerloo from 1977 onwards. Following the separation from the Jubilee line, they have monopolised the Bakerloo service. In 2024 they were the oldest passenger stock on London Underground.

The short-lived Charing Cross Jubilee line station sees a 1972 Mk II train awaiting departure for Wembley Park. Everything may look right, but sadly the railway was in the wrong place. The overrun tunnels extended most of the way to Aldwych for the intended continuation to Fleet Street and beyond, but the immediate objectives turned out to be Westminster, Waterloo, London Bridge and, as we now know, Docklands.

This is a Jubilee line train of 1996 stock arriving from Stratford at West Ham, shortly after its opening in January 1998. It was photographed from the North London line platforms, then still host to third rail DC EMUs between Richmond and North Woolwich. These are now used by Docklands Light Railway services, Stratford to Woolwich Arsenal or Beckton.

This is an internal view of the 1996 stock, showing how transverse seats have by now been displaced by an all-longitudinal seating arrangement. Also noticeable is the number of vertical handholds, which are well spread out. These can make the lot of those who have to stand considerably easier, especially if the driver has to make a sudden brake application.

The somewhat contorted trackwork seen here on all the lines north of West Ham, with a westbound Jubilee line train, was the result of making the best possible use of the inherited infrastructure without incurring excessive costs. What were then North London line tracks on the right have since been acquired and reused by the Docklands Light Railway.

North of West Ham station, the line on the left leads to Stratford Market depot and the 1996 stock train disappearing under the bridge is en route for Stratford itself. The very substantial fence that keeps the North London services separate from those of the Jubilee line is notable; how much physical protection for the trackside staff of each undertaking needs to be given?

Northern Line

Morden depot for the Northern line sees two clean 1972 Mk I stock trains on 3 May 1990. There are thirty-two depot roads here, which have to supply a goodly proportion of the daily train usage. How might matters work out should the Northern be split into two separate lines of via Bank and via Charing Cross, with one of them taking the Edgware branch and the other High Barnet?

Two 1959 stock trains are joined in Morden depot by the London Transport Museum's four-car 1938 stock train on one of its periodic outings in November 1990. The Northern was operated entirely by 1938 stock for many years, but it also found long-term use on the Bakerloo (with a pre-1938 additional trailer) and, in modest numbers, the Piccadilly.

The running tunnels approaching the Northern's Morden terminus lead almost immediately to three tracks and five platforms. The tracks continue (left) to the depot only. This was a full house scene in May 1990. The ability to run an intensive service depends crucially on the speed of reversing the trains at termini and constant attention to timekeeping.

Tooting Bec station is a Charles Holden design and is typical of those built new south of Clapham Common for the Morden extension of the Northern line. With its Portland stone finish, it was opened on 13 September 1926. The positioning on a crossroad corner meant that everybody could see it from all directions and the station itself became an advertisement for the undertaking.

Kennington station retains much of its original charm. Dating from the opening of the City &
South London Railway, later the Northern line, on 18 December 1890, the dome was built to
accommodate the lift mechanisms needed to take the passengers from street to platform level.
This is the only remaining example of its type and was seen here in December 1996.

This signal at Borough on 27 January 2000
is an example of a repeater displayed to train
guards, so that they know if the driver has right
of way. In this case, he has. Signalling the driver
(by bell) when station duties are complete,
without the right of way, would be potentially
dangerous if the driver took it as his authority
to start.

On 1959 stock trains, guards were positioned at the front of the last coach. A smartly turned-out individual is seen here at Borough on the final day these trains were used before withdrawal. The date is 27 January 2000. Something like forty years of daily service is a good life for vehicles of this nature; they were replaced by the Northern's 1995 stock trains.

This London Bridge Northern line platform has lost its track but gained extra platform area, while the old tunnel entrance has been crudely hidden (for the time being). This was part of the work to create a new concourse to cope with the extra traffic that the Jubilee line, then under construction, was likely to create.

Angel station on the City branch of the Northern line sees a northbound 1959 stock train with a working to Mill Hill East. A narrow island platform with a width of 3.7 metres in total was less than ideal for this busy station. In 1992 the northbound line was diverted to a new parallel tunnel with its own platform. Escalators replaced lifts and there was a new station entrance.

A southbound train to Morden of 1959 stock arrives at the un-rebuilt Angel in March 1987. Access to the platform was then available only by stairs from the northern end – seen here. The only remaining examples of such a layout with a narrow island platform are at Clapham North and Clapham Common Northern line stations, for the time being anyway.

On the Edgware branch of the Northern, the line emerges into the daylight just short of Golders Green, the original terminus of 1907. A 1959 stock train makes for the southbound (central) tunnel in May 1990. The furthest left tunnel is only a headshunt, essential for use by trains going to or from the depot, also on that side of the line but not visible.

North of Golders Green but short of Brent Cross, the line crosses the two parts of Pelier Rise. This road had to be severed and houses demolished to allow the railway to be constructed in 1923, at a relatively high level. This followed the continuing delays in building the Edgware extension. A 1959 stock train forms a southbound service in June 1990.

Brent Cross, renamed from Brent on 20 July 1976, sees northbound and southbound Northern line trains crossing in August 1990. At one time there were two passing tracks here, the remains of which can just be discerned, so that fast services could overtake the 'all stations'. Interwar aspirations, like the nine-car as well as seven-car trains, did not survive the Second World War.

On the High Barnet branch, the outstanding feature is Eric Aumonier's sculpture *Forward* at
East Finchley, first served by the Underground on 3 July 1939. As matters turned out, the only
Underground route forward from here was that via Camden Town, the former Great Northern
route to Finsbury Park being abandoned. Or could it have referred also to the trolleybuses on
the road below?

New facilities at Highgate were partly constructed, as this picture of September 1999 shows. The track bed for what would have been northbound services has been filled in. This route, however, was used to transfer Underground rolling stock for overhaul from Drayton Park depot to Acton Works, until this ceased due to the worsening condition of the infrastructure.

What might have been described as Highgate low level (a name never used) was opened on 19 January 1941. Trains had been passing through here without stopping since 1 July 1939, when the Northern was extended to East Finchley. This is not to be confused with the original Highgate tube line terminus, which in consequence was renamed Archway.

On the route to Finsbury Park, Highgate Hill would have to be surmounted or tunnels would need to be driven beneath it. The railway chose the latter course and the southern end of two single-line bores are seen here. There is no public access, despite the apparent footpath to one of them. Main-line services from Finsbury Park used to continue through these tunnels to Edgware, High Barnet or Alexandra Palace.

The station at Crouch End was partly reconstructed by London Transport under the New Works proposals, but little of any real consequence was achieved. The last passenger trains it was to see were those for the Alexandra Palace branch, which closed permanently on 5 July 1954. Much of the route does, however, make an attractive public walkway.

The surface route south from East Finchley might have led to Drayton Park, which was on the Underground line from Moorgate to Finsbury Park. This became part of British Railways and No. 313.055 dual voltage unit in Network SouthEast livery is seen leaving for the Great Northern line on a Down train on 22 April 1998. The Up line emerges from the tunnel on the right – note the platform curvature.

The Northern line mainstay of many years, a 1938 stock train arrives at Finchley Central from High Barnet in August 1976, with a train for Kennington via Charing Cross. It was important for the route to be displayed on the front of the train to try and ensure passengers got on the one that they wanted. Scurrying around Camden Town, or a much longer walk at Euston, was not a good idea!

The 1972 Mk I stock had unpainted doors, which enabled them to be distinguished quickly from their Mk II counterparts with red doors. Based very much on the 1967 stock design produced for the Victoria line, but crew operated and without automatic train operation, a train of the Mk I stock for Morden via Bank is arriving at Finchley Central from the Mill Hill East branch.

The Mill Hill East branch was in the course of being converted to a double-track route to Edgware, but work never progressed beyond the stage reached in 1941. A 1959 stock train, bequeathed to the Northern when the Piccadilly received new 1973 stock, is approaching the terminus in October 1995. The Northern gained an unenviable reputation for being the home for other people's cast-offs.

A southbound 1938 stock train is seen at Lovers Walk Bridge between West Finchley and Finchley Central on a Morden via Charing Cross service. It is early 1977 and the remains of some snowfall can be seen at the trackside. It always seems that both gradients and curvature on Underground lines that were once part of the National Rail system are rather easier.

Interwar housing expansion resulted in the LNER building a station at West Finchley. Opened on 1 March 1933, it used several fitments retrieved from earlier station closures. The line was transferred to London Underground on 14 April 1940. A southbound 1938 stock train for Morden via Bank is seen arriving beneath the reconstructed road overbridge.

This is an interior view of the guard's position on 1938 stock Driving Motor Car No. 11182, as displayed in the London Transport Museum. The door controls are duplicated on each side and the horizontal bar, marked 'Guard Only', was aimed at keeping others out. In reality, between stations the guard usually sat on the first upholstered seat in the saloon and the bar was rarely raised.

A local resident, the comedian Spike Milligan (1918–2002) of *Goon Show* fame, was said to have inspired the repainting of Woodside Park 'to brighten the whole place up'. A seven-car train of 1959 stock is arriving on a southbound service for Kennington via Charing Cross on 6 June 1977. The footbridge was for public use as well as passengers, so there were, nominally, ticket barriers on both platforms.

Woodside Park had all the trappings of a real country station, barring the fourth rail electrification and the colour light signals. This view is looking north towards the High Barnet terminus on 24 April 1997. The former Great Northern Railway signal box dated from the line's opening in 1872, though it was not being used for such purposes, having been replaced as long ago as 1906.

Piccadilly Line

The Rayners Lane to Uxbridge section regularly sees both tube and subsurface trains on its tracks, with the attendant problems of different floor heights in the rolling stock and what that means for stepping distances. A 1973 stock train is leaving Hillingdon station in February 1997 and crossing the A40–M40 link road by the new bridge.

Sudbury Town station was rebuilt by Charles Holden in a completely new style and was finished in 1931. It featured a brick box with a flat concrete roof; other derivative designs would appear in the years leading up to the Second World War. Modernity extended to the whole station, including the ticket hall and the footbridge linking the two tracks. This is a September 1999 view.

The roundels survived at Sudbury Town, even if their width had to be compressed to fit the space available. This picture shows how it could be done. Corporate styles can be hard taskmasters; deviate too far from the promoted image and the result ends up not being recognised by, or pleasing, anybody.

A novel addition at Sudbury Town inside and on the left of the ticket hall for those arriving for their trains was this barometer. Indicating a 'changeable' reading when photographed in September 1999, hurrying passengers were perhaps at least as interested in the clock on the right-hand wall, which was opposite.

This is the view of an approaching 1973 stock Piccadilly line train from the present westbound platform at Hounslow West. This was originally an above ground terminal station which had been reconstructed in 1925–31. Large-scale rebuilding was needed when the line was extended to serve what would eventually become the four Heathrow Airport stations.

Fly the Tube to Heathrow

Services by the supersonic airliner Concorde were launched on 21 January 1976. The slightly less than supersonic Piccadilly line reached what was then Heathrow Central on 16 December 1977. This is a 1987 poster, *Take Off*, from a painting commissioned by London Underground from Wilson McLean. Concorde's last commercial flight was on 24 November 2003.

An eastbound departure from Osterley shows the curve that all trains have to negotiate and a 1973 stock train doing just that. For such journeys the driver needs camera back up, as that is the only way he can observe the doors from the centre to the rear of his train. That problem does not occur on the westbound line; the situation at each station needs to be taken on its merits.

This apparently rural scene is of a 1973 stock train on the Piccadilly line approaching Boston Manor, the station buildings of which are on the A3002 at the western end of Northfields depot. It is August 1990. A total of eighty-eight of these trains were built by Metro-Cammell and the 17.5-metre-long vehicles were designed to be rather better than their predecessors in accommodating airport passengers' luggage.

This interior view of a 1973 stock train for the Piccadilly shows how an increase in the stand back position at the sliding doors could, at least theoretically, add to the space in which luggage could be stowed. To what extent passengers might be inclined to leave it there while they sought an available seat is another matter, but at least the designers tried.

Lights are lit and it will soon be completely dark at South Ealing, as an eastbound Piccadilly line train approaches in October 1987. While there are four tracks, that on the far right – the eastbound local – was normally used for test running only. From here to Northfields, whose station building can be seen in the distance, is a mere 0.38 km.

This is the eastern end of South Ealing station with a Piccadilly line train of 1973 stock train in corporate colours arriving. The station itself is what might be termed part-modernised; the canopy on the right is much more accommodating than the restricted facilities on the left. But perhaps that reflects the direction in which most passengers want to go.

Nearest the camera is a 1973 stock Piccadilly line train entering the turn back siding west of Acton Town station. It is meeting an eastbound train coming from the Heathrow direction. The line connecting to the higher level is for eastbound District line trains from Ealing Broadway or Piccadilly from Uxbridge. Some D stock trains can be seen in the depot at the top of the picture. It is 18 April 1990.

1973 stock trains on the fast lines, both in pre-corporate livery, meet at the eastern end of Acton Town station on 18 April 1990. A certain amount of shuffling can be necessary here, to separate Piccadilly trains continuing towards Heathrow or Rayners Lane and Uxbridge, and District services for Ealing Broadway or towards Westminster. There is also the complication of the fast lines and the local lines.

Stamford Brook, seen here, has an island platform for the use of westbound services, but for the eastbound only the local line has a platform. A necessarily non-stop Piccadilly on the westbound fast hurries through the station in November 1997. Of note is the remarkably high-level colour light signal; presumably station canopies would otherwise obstruct the driver's vision.

Arnos Grove station dates from the expansion of the Piccadilly line north of Finsbury Park, and services commenced on 19 September 1932. The 'drum' architecture was another much-admired Charles Holden work, and the building is now Grade II listed. Facilities were provided for tram services and are now used by buses. This view was taken on 24 April 1997.

Arnos Grove station was provided additionally with a central platform for terminating trains. This is useful if traffic levels make it unnecessary to continue the further 5 km to Cockfosters, either by design or as a correcting move following service disruption. Here a 1973 stock train to Heathrow is arriving from the northern terminus on 24 April 1997.

Southgate station is in tunnels made up of twin tubes, but these are only 849 metres long. An eastbound 1973 stock train for Cockfosters is seen emerging in July 1989. The tunnels enabled the line to be taken below the road junction in the central shopping street area; again, the station incorporates a bus terminal. The line was extended as far as Oakwood on 13 March 1933.

The general dimensions of Oakwood, the last but one station on the eastbound Piccadilly, bears a distinct reminder of the Sudbury Town architecture. The station did not acquire this name until 1946, having been known as Enfield West since and opening in 1933. Local politics can be unforgiving in their pursuit of correctness. Note the station trading, as exemplified by the flower shop.

The Piccadilly line to Cockfosters was opened on 31 July 1933. This view is of a train arriving at Platform 4. Again, there are three tracks but four platforms, the centre track having a platform on each side. Selective door opening can allow flows of arriving departing passengers to be kept separate, should the volumes of each so warrant.

Cockfosters station is next to the A111 road. On the opposite (west) side of that road is this impressive waiting shelter for bus passengers; steps inside take them to (or from) the Underground concourse. Should the Underground have been extended further? Possibly, but this was (and remains) largely undeveloped land with titles such as Beech Hill Park, as well as a golf course.

Victoria Line

As part of an exhibition to mark fifty years of London Transport on 2/3 July 1983 at Acton Works, a 1967 stock Driving Motor from the Victoria line was on display. No parts of the Victoria line open to the public are above ground, so this was an opportunity to find out what these trains really looked like. As it turned out, the main noticeable difference was in the lack of provision for a guard.

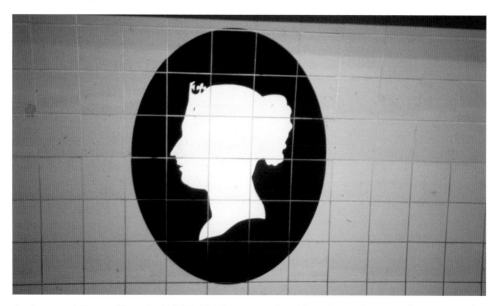

An image of Queen Victoria (1837–1901) was used at Victoria Underground station and is displayed in all the recesses above the station's platform seating. Images of relevance to the location are provided at all sixteen stations on the line; some are mildly tongue-in-cheek, with Warren Street represented by a maze. The line itself was opened by Elizabeth II on 7 March 1969.

This is a 1967 stock train led by Driving Motor No. 3153 in corporate livery moving round Northumberland Park depot on 24 April 1997. The wrap-around cab windows may give the driver something approaching all-round vision and at the same time look attractive, but they are an expensive item to replace if and when they get broken.

This is the full length of a Victoria line 1967 stock train at Northumberland Park depot, shortly to take up a duty on the line. End-to-end running times are about 30 minutes, and the line is 21.25 km in length from Walthamstow to Brixton. Staff trains run between Seven Sisters and the depot Staff Platform if there are no regular timed workings entering or leaving the depot.

Waterloo & City line

The Armstrong lift was used to lower and raise the Waterloo & City stock to and from the system, but it disappeared under what became Waterloo International. Southern Railway car No. S55 of 1940 stock, in British Railways blue livery with grey doors plus a Network SouthEast label, is seen in the then sidings on the west side of the main-line station in February 1987.

This London Underground 1992 stock look-a-like on the Waterloo & City line has set down its passengers at Bank on 28 December 1996. It is still in Network SouthEast livery, despite having been part of the Underground from 1994. This 2-km railway was opened on 8 August 1898 by an offshoot of the London & South Western to take their passengers from Waterloo to the City, which is still its principal purpose.

In 1998 the Waterloo & City reached its centenary and the Waterloo depot was opened to the public on 8 August. This is the inspection pit, with a Driving Motor Car raised above it. There are ten two-car units made up into five four-car trains to provide all services. Maximum speed of the stock is 100 km/h, but this is not needed on a journey that takes around 4 minutes from one terminus to the other.

Engineering Trains

In 1976 London Underground's Acton Works created a Tunnel Cleaning Train of five vehicles. The end cars were from redundant 1938 stock. Moving at 0.5 mph, it used high-pressure hoses in the centre car to dislodge the accumulated general filth from the tunnels. This was sucked into the cars on either side for later disposal. The aim was to improve the environment for passengers and staff alike.

No. L11 was an Acton Works shunter, constructed in 1964 from a pair of Standard stock vehicles of 1931. This produced two cabs and two sets of controls, back-to-back. For ease of maintenance, traction equipment was moved from the underframe to what had been passenger accommodation. Couplings for sub-surface and tube stock were fitted at the Acton Works end; tube stock was only at the other.

Battery-electric locomotives have long been the mainstay of haulage power on the Underground for works trains of all sorts. Constructed to tube gauge, they could be used throughout the system. This is No. L25 of the TransPlant fleet, built by Metro-Cammell as part of a batch of thirteen and delivered in 1965. It is seen here at an Old Oak Common open day on 6 February 2000.

Battery locomotive Nos L28 (nearer) and L52 (further) are in both in a condition that emphasises their need to work for a living. It is 15 March 1997 at Ruislip. No. L28 is one of a build of thirteen Metro-Cammell vehicles in 1964/65; No. L52 came from eleven built by British Railways, Doncaster, in 1973/74. All comply with tube loading-gauge requirements and can be coupled with standard main-line vehicles.

Electric Sleet Locomotives were an important part of the Underground back-up fleet. They were built from pairs of redundant Motor Cars, joined back-to-back. This is No. ESL117, seen at Neasden on 24 April 1983. Two de-icing bogies in the centre of the car carried ice cutters to clear the conductor rails, to which anti-freeze solution was then applied. By 1985, all eighteen had been replaced by de-icing gear fitted to service trains.

On show at Acton Works in 1983 are (left to right) Q38 sub-surface Driving Motor Cars, originally Nos 4416/7, but now Nos L126/7. As pilot cars, they were used for moving other vehicles around the system. Next are tube pilot cars, Nos L130/1 of 1934, and Electric Sleet Locomotive ESL No. 107. This was converted from a pair of Central London cars in 1939.

Museums and Preservation

No. 12 *Sarah Siddons* is a Metropolitan electric locomotive dating from 1922/23. Built (or technically rebuilt) by Metropolitan-Vickers at Barrow-in-Furness, these locomotives had a 1-hour rating of 1,200 hp and a top speed of 65 mph. No longer required for revenue work following electrification to Amersham, No. 12 remains a regular performer at heritage events.

The fleet of twenty Metropolitan Railway locomotives were each a modest 39 feet 6 inches (12.03 metres) long. They were named in 1927, mostly after people with some connection with the area served. The plaque on No. 12 *Sarah Siddons* reads: 'In August 1973, this locomotive took part in the exhibition and cavalcade to commemorate the 150th anniversary of the Stockton & Darlington Railway.' That was more than 200 miles away.

This is Driving Motor Car No. 4248 of Q23 stock, as withdrawn from the District line in 1971. Built in 1923 by Gloucester Railway Carriage & Wagon Co., it originally had manual sliding doors that were operated by passengers. Latterly these were replaced by air-operated ones, under the control of the guard. It is seen at the London Transport Museum, Covent Garden.

Metropolitan No. 23 of 1866, later No. L45, but subsequently No. 23 again, was one of a whole series of similar 4-4-0T steam locomotives purchased by the Metropolitan Railway. Beyer Peacock were the builders. It is seen here with Northern line 1938 Driving Motor Car No. 11182 at the London Transport Museum in June 1990. Both are very static.

Between 1956 and 1963, London Transport acquired a total of thirteen Great Western 0-6-0 Pannier Tanks from British Railways for engineering work, replacing their own ageing fleet. Several were subsequently preserved; this is No. L99 built in 1930 (previously BR No. 7715) at the Buckinghamshire Railway Centre, Quainton Road, in April 1998.

No. DL83 is a Sentinel diesel hydraulic, one of three acquired by London Transport in 1971. Unfortunately, their wheelbase was too short to operate track circuits reliably on their own and it was feared that they were too heavy to negotiate some of the bridges. As a result, their use other than within Neasden or Lillie Bridge depots was rather limited. DL83 is seen here at the Nene Valley Railway.

Island Line

Ryde Pier Head station seen here once had four platforms. Although there are still two, that serving the shuttle to Ryde Esplanade is long-term disused. One platform and the single track to Ryde Esplanade are now seen as sufficient. A 1938 stock train with No. 483.005 leading awaits its ferry passengers from Portsmouth before departing on the 8-mile twenty-nine chains to Shanklin.

The first electric trains on the Island line were those of London Underground's pre-1938 stock converted to third rail. Here, No. 485.045 leads its train into Pier Head station in May 1988. They were responsible for all services from 1967 until replaced by 1938 stock in 1989/90. The sight of elderly London Underground electric trains negotiating a thirty-two-chain-long (704 yards) railway on a pier always seemed a little odd!

On 2 October 1986 No. 485.045, a five-car formation of a 4VEC unit, plus a trailer from a 3TIS, leaves Ryde St John's Road for Ryde Pier Head. Vectis was the Roman name for the island. The forty-three cars, which in 1967 it was thought would be needed to run the island system, shrank to eighteen when replaced by the 1938 stock in 1989. It is now down to ten cars with the Class 464s, former District D stock of 1978.

Ryde St John's Road is a
tunnel length and 0.75 miles
away from the Esplanade. It is
the centre of the Island system.
Here, a pre-1938 stock train
formed of No. 485.041
with mixed liveries arrives
with a train from Shanklin.
Semaphore signals were still
in control here in October
1980. The front of the
train is in British Railways
colours, while the rear is in
Network SouthEast.

A 1938 stock train with
No. 485.005 in Network
SouthEast livery en route
for Ryde Pier Head arrives
at Brading on 17 June
1992. Single tracking here
restricted line capacity to
a 20/40-minute frequency,
which didn't even vaguely
match ferry services
operating every half hour.
On privatisation in 1984,
Sealink ferries had ceased to
be part of British Railways.

The interior of the 1938 stock
trains was changed little,
although fluorescent strip
lights replaced the traditional
bulbs in their holders. All
vehicles of what became the
nine examples of Class 483
are pairs of Driving Motor
Cars, with that at the north
end carrying the guard's
control panels as seen here
in 1992. This is No. 483.007
(or plain 007 as seen on the
panel). Note the retained
tip-up seats, an impediment to
quick joining and alighting.

Pre-1938 stock set No. 485.041 is providing a Ryde Pier Head to Shanklin train. It stands in Sandown's Down platform in July 1988, awaiting the arrival of the Up train on the single track from Shanklin. The scene is overlooked by the impressive signal box, but this did not survive the track singling between here and Brading. The passing loop and a few sidings remain.

No. 485.045 stands at the Shanklin terminus on 2 October 1988. A bid under the government's Restoring Your Railway programme to again reach Ventnor (and Newport) was rejected in January 2023. Not the least of the Ventnor problems is the remoteness of the old station site from the town itself. The proposers' aspirations were described by a commentator as 'a hopeless fantasy'.

Way Out

It needs to be made clear to customers how to leave the premises in the normal course of events, as well as in a case of major disruption or even emergency. The illuminated 'Way Out' sign at the bottom of the bank of escalators at St John's Wood uses the near-universal recognition of the roundel to give authority to that very basic message.

Bibliography

The following works contain reference material of general interest and use. Others, including Wikipedia and books too numerous to mention here, cover the history and development of the system.

Brown, Joe, *London Railway Atlas*, Fourth Edition (Ian Allan Publishing, 2015)

Glover, John, *London's Underground*, Twelfth Edition (Ian Allan Publishing, 2015)

Hardy, Brian, *London Underground Rolling Stock* (Capital Transport, 2002)

Menear, Laurence, *London Underground Stations: A Social and Architectural Study* (Midas Books, 1983)

Munsey, Myles (ed.), *Railway Track Diagrams Book 5: Southern & TfL*, Fourth Edition (TRACKmaps, 2019)

Quick, M. E., *Railway Passenger Stations in England, Scotland and Wales: A Chronology*, Third Edition (Railway & Canal Historical Society, 2005)

Rose, Douglas, *The London Underground: A Diagrammatic History*, Tenth Edition (distributed by Capital Transport, 2022)